D1270551

Why did
THE RISE OF THE NAZIS
happen?

CHARLES FREEMAN

Gareth Stevens
Publishing

Please visit our Web site, www.garethstevens.com.
For a free color catalog of all our high-quality books,
call toll free 1-800-542-2595 or fax 1-877-542-2596.

Library of Congress Cataloging-in-Publication Data

Freeman, Charles, 1947-
  Why did the rise of the Nazis happen? / Charles
Freeman.
      p. cm.
  Includes index.
  ISBN 978-1-4339-4175-7 (library binding)
  ISBN 978-1-4339-4176-4 (pbk.)
  ISBN 978-1-4339-4177-1 (6-pack)
  1. Germany—Politics and government—1918-1933—
Juvenile literature. 2. National socialism—Juvenile
literature. 3. Hitler, Adolf, 1889-1945—Juvenile
literature. I. Title.
  DD240.F724 2011
  943.085—dc22
                  2010017229

First Edition

Published in 2011 by
Gareth Stevens Publishing
111 East 14th Street, Suite 349
New York, NY 10003

Copyright © 2011 Arcturus Publishing

Series concept: Alex Woolf
Editors: Rebecca Gerlings and Philip de Ste. Croix
Designer: Andrew Easton
Picture researcher: Thomas Mitchell
Project manager: Joe Harris

Photo credits: All images copyright of Getty Images,
except cover image: Bettmann/Corbis and page 7:
Corbis.

Printed in the United States of America

CPSIA compliance information: Batch #AS10GS: For further information contact
Gareth Stevens, New York, New York at 1-800-542-2595.

SL001512US

CONTENTS

CHAPTER 1

THE PAIN OF DEFEAT

January 30, 1933, was a momentous day in German history. A new chancellor was appointed—Adolf Hitler, the leader of the Nazi Party. One of the cornerstones of Hitler's Nazi philosophy was the restoration of German power through a political strategy that emphasized the importance of race, authority, and the right of the German people to expand to the east by taking land from the "inferior" Slav peoples. Inside Germany, political enemies, notably Communists and Jews, would be hunted out of public life. Nazi rule unfolded during the 1930s like a living nightmare. Eventually, all of Europe would descend into war while Jewish people were taken away and deliberately exterminated.

The changes in Germany came about mainly because of the defeat it suffered in World War I. Armistice Day on November 11, 1918, marked the end of one of the most terrible wars in history. For four years, the major nations of Europe had fought for supremacy in a bitter and costly conflict. Germany, a strong and powerful nation, had fought its huge neighbor, Russia, to a standstill. It had occupied large parts of northern France in the course of the campaigns. However, France and its ally, Great Britain, had hung on in the face of terrible casualties. They had held fast against the Germans in the trenches of the Western Front. Then the Allies fought off a final German offensive in the summer of 1918, with the help of a new ally, the United States, and the German armies began to fall back. To the east, Germany's allies,

This is the shattered entrance of the Royal Palace in Berlin, the German capital. It was attacked and damaged by looting workers during the Communist uprisings of 1919. The German middle class felt shocked and threatened by the civil disturbances and longed for a leader who would restore order and strong government.

Bulgaria and Austria-Hungary, were defeated. German morale collapsed and the German generals conceded defeat.

The country felt shocked and humiliated. The ships of Germany's High Seas Fleet had to be surrendered to the Allies, the army was driven back into Germany, and people faced starvation as food supplies were blockaded. Soon rumors were circulating that Germany had not been defeated, but that its army had been sabotaged by enemies of the state, such as revolutionaries or Jews. The country itself was never occupied, and this encouraged the belief that defeat had somehow come from within. The leaders who had signed the armistice were dubbed "the November Criminals." The government, which had been led by two generals, Paul von Hindenburg and Erich Ludendorff, collapsed, and Kaiser Wilhelm II, Germany's emperor, fled to Holland.

THE THREAT OF COMMUNISM

Inspired by the example of the recent Russian Revolution of 1917, Communist uprisings by groups of workers took place in many major German cities.

On February 11, 1919, Friedrich Ebert was elected president of the Weimar Republic—a position he held until his death in 1925. Here he is being sworn in.

This photograph shows the German delegates gathered at Versailles for the signing of the treaty. Germany was outraged when the terms of the Versailles Treaty were made known. However, it became clear that the country would either have to swallow its pride and sign, or risk war breaking out again.

Panic spread among the middle class, who felt that the traditional social framework was under threat. Friedrich Ebert, the leader of the Social Democrats, a moderate workers' party, was able to restore order by 1920 with the help of the army and the Freikorps, bands of young men and ex-soldiers formed to help patrol the streets. The Freikorps were sometimes undisciplined, but the middle class was prepared to overlook any shortcomings when Communists were their target. Street fighting between rival armed bands now became a commonplace feature of everyday life.

Ebert's government managed to restore some stability and then drew up a new constitution. Germany was to be a republic, known as the Weimar Republic after the town where the constitution was written. Monarchy would not be restored. Instead, a president would be elected by popular vote every seven years. The center of power was the parliament, the Reichstag. Elections would be decided by proportional representation. Electors would vote for their chosen party, and seats for the deputies, or members of the Reichstag, would be distributed according to the number of votes that each party managed to attract. If thirty-three percent voted for the Social Democrats, for example, they would receive a third of the seats.

A Berlin policeman reads a wall poster ordering German civilians to surrender their arms in accordance with the Treaty of Versailles.

National shame

The German delegation to Versailles was not involved in the treaty negotiations. On May 7, 1919, it was simply presented with the final text. The delegation was horrified by what it saw. "Germany cannot accept these terms and live with honor as a nation," said the head of the delegation. But the Allies threatened to renew the war if Germany did not sign the treaty. Eventually, the Germans had no choice but to accept it, and on May 28, the delegation signed. "It was the worst hour of my life," said one delegate.

This process became confusing because so many political parties contested the election. The Social Democrats, who represented the vast majority of German workers, wanted peaceful progress toward a workers' state. The Communist Party, however, was prepared for violent revolution. The two parties were in a battle for the workers' votes. The Center Party had close links with the Catholic Church. On the other side of the spectrum, conservatives, especially those in rural areas, longed for a return to prewar Germany and the old order of kaiser and landowners. They voted for the National People's Party. Other smaller

World War I was the first war in which air power had been used extensively, largely for reconnaissance. As part of the Treaty of Versailles, Germany was forced to disband its air force. This picture shows the scrapping of those planes that remained.

parties represented a range of other views. It was difficult for any one party to gain an overall majority. Alliances, or coalitions, were formed with other parties to try to gain an advantage. It was established that if the parties of the Reichstag failed to form a government, then the president could break the logjam and rule on his own authority by decree. He could even order in the army to restore order. Thus, from the very beginning of the Weimar Republic, it was possible for a strong president to overturn parliamentary democracy.

CONTROVERSIAL PEACE TERMS

The first job facing the new republic was how to draw up a peace settlement. The new government hoped that the victorious Allies would show some sympathy toward them because they had established a democracy in place of a military government. However, when the Allies met to conclude a peace treaty at Versailles—the former French royal palace outside Paris—they showed no mercy. Germany and its allies were declared guilty of causing the war, and this meant that Germany had to make a large reparation payment for the damage it had caused. The German army was reduced to 100,000 men and its aircraft were scrapped. The French in particular wanted revenge for their suffering. Germany had to be punished and its forces made weak. To secure France's borders, German troops were barred from the Rhineland, the territory running alongside the French frontier. The German borders with the new state of Poland, which was carved out of the former Russian empire, were drawn in Poland's favor. All of Germany's colonies in foreign countries were confiscated. Thirteen percent of the country's land area and ten percent of its people were taken away. The signing of the Versailles treaty on June 28, 1919, was a day of national shame for Germany. The mood of resentment was so strong that any politician who promised to overturn it would be guaranteed a sympathetic ear.

Public anger at the terms of the Treaty of Versailles led to mass demonstrations, such as this assembly in Munich in early June 1919.

Was Versailles unjust?

Debate over whether the Versailles treaty was too harsh has continued to rage since it was first signed. The British economist J. M. Keynes was a powerful critic in 1920:

"The policy of reducing Germany to servitude for a generation, of degrading the lives of millions of human beings, and of depriving a whole nation of happiness should be abhorrent and detestable."

Modern historian Richard Evans takes a different view.

"The reparations bills . . . were not beyond the country's resources to meet and not unreasonable given the wanton destruction visited upon Belgium and France by the occupying German armies."

J. M. Keynes, *The Economic Causes of the Peace* (Harcourt, Brace and Howe, 1920); Richard Evans, *The Coming of the Third Reich* (Allen Lane, Penguin, 2003)

CHAPTER 2

HITLER'S POWER GROWS

Adolf Hitler was in a hospital recovering from the effects of a gas attack when the news broke of Germany's defeat. He was a 29-year-old Austrian who had been serving in the German army during World War I. His sense of shock was profound. He later described his reaction to the news of Germany's defeat: "I threw myself on the cot and buried my burning head in the covers. . . . And so it had all been in vain. . . . Did all this war happen so that a gang of wretched criminals could lay hands on the fatherland? . . . In these nights hatred grew in me, hatred for those responsible for this deed." Hitler vowed that he would destroy those who had brought Germany to its knees.

ADOLF HITLER'S BACKGROUND

Adolf Hitler was born in Braunau am Inn in Austria on April 20, 1889. Hitler's mother, Klara, was the third wife of Alois Hitler, a customs official who worked on the border between Austria and Germany. He was a cold and reserved man. Klara, twenty-three years his junior, was dominated by him. Alois died in 1903. In 1905, Hitler left home for Vienna, the capital of the Austro-Hungarian empire. He wanted to study as a painter at the Academy of Fine Arts, but his application was

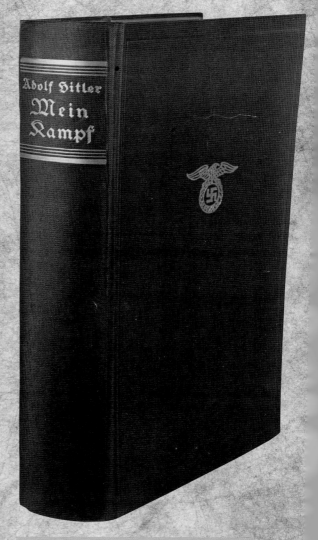

Hitler wrote much of *Mein Kampf* while in prison. Part autobiography, part political testament, it became the bible of the Nazi movement.

turned down twice. Instead, Hitler drifted between cheap lodging houses in the city. The death of his mother from cancer in December 1907 upset him deeply.

Rootless and lacking friends, Hitler brooded on what had gone wrong with his life and who was to blame. In his autobiography, *Mein Kampf (My Struggle)*, he later explained how he came to the conclusion that the Jews were responsible for the evils of the world. Anti-Semitism (deep prejudice against Jews that was based on their race and their religion) was common in Europe at this time. Many Christians still blamed the Jews for Christ's death, while others identified Jewish speculators as being the people who wielded the real power in the newly industrialized age. Hitler's anti-Semitism grew into an obsession. He scorned the "racial inferiority" of Jews and poured hatred on them. He wrote: "Wherever I went, I now saw Jews, and the more I saw, the more sharply they set themselves apart in my eyes from the rest of humanity. . . . Was there any

Hitler as a schoolboy

No one could have guessed the future that the young Adolf Hitler had ahead of him. Professor Eduard Humer, one of his schoolteachers, remembered his pupil in this way:

"I can recall the gaunt, pale-faced youth pretty well. He had definite talent, though in a narrow field. But he lacked self-discipline, being notoriously quarrelsome, willful, arrogant and irascible … his enthusiasm for hard work evaporated all too quickly.

"He reacted with ill-concealed hostility to advice or reproof; at the same time he demanded of his fellow pupils their unqualified subservience, fancying himself in the role of leader."

Franz Jetzinger, *Hitler's Youth* (Greenwood Press, 1977)

Hitler was among the crowds in the Odeon Platz in Munich cheering the news of the outbreak of war in August 1914. He had arrived in Munich from Austria the year before.

Adolf Hitler (on the right) with two fellow soldiers at a military hospital in April 1915. Hitler never rose higher than the rank of corporal in the army, but his war record was good and he was even awarded a medal for bravery. He also apparently enjoyed the comradeship of army life after enduring years of loneliness while living in Vienna.

Party. Hitler got involved in the political argument in such an effective way that he was asked to become a member of the executive committee that ran the party.

Like many other Germans, he was striving to find a role in the new Germany. Hitler suddenly realized that he had a gift for public speaking. He sympathized with the feelings of the audiences who came to listen to the German Workers' Party. The Treaty of Versailles had just been signed and the German economy was in ruins. Hitler argued that someone must take the

form of filth or profligacy, particularly in cultural life, without at least one Jew involved in it?"

In 1913, Hitler moved from Austria to Munich, the capital of the southern German state of Bavaria. He then joined the German army when war was declared in 1914. His duties were not without risk—he was a runner between the trenches—and he was awarded an Iron Cross for bravery.

A PERSUASIVE VOICE

Hitler remained in the army for some time after the war. In Munich, the military was used to keep an eye on the many small revolutionary parties, and in September 1919, Hitler was sent to check up on a meeting of a group calling themselves the German Workers'

VOICES FROM HISTORY

Getting the message across

Hitler was a brilliantly effective at manipulating his audiences:

"The receptivity of the great masses is very limited, their intelligence is small, but their power of forgetting is enormous. In consequence of these facts, all effective propaganda must be limited to a very few points and must harp on these in slogans until the last member of the public understands what you want him to understand."

Adolf Hitler, *Mein Kampf* (Lightning Source UK Ltd., 2004)

blame, and that the German people must be reborn and fight back against their enemies—notably the Jews and Communists. Over the next few months, more and more people came to hear him speak. They were fascinated by what he had to say.

HITLER TAKES CHARGE

The party was soon to get a new identity. In February 1920, it became the National Socialist German Workers' Party, a name that was shortened to Nazis. Bit by bit, organization and structure were put in place, and by July 1921 Hitler was very evidently its leader. He set out a program of twenty-five demands, including the abolition of the Treaty of Versailles, the establishment of a greater Germany uniting all Germans in possession of enough land to feed all its peoples, and the ending of civil rights for Jews. An ancient sign, the swastika, was chosen as the symbol of the party. It was depicted in black, red, and white, the

In the 1920s, many German political groups kept bodyguard detachments of loyal followers to maintain order at meetings. This small group of SA members are described as "Hitler's Shock Troops."

In 1923, the value of the German currency plummeted while the price of goods increased dramatically. The German mark in effect lost all its value. Prices eventually reached a billion times what they had been in 1914. At the height of this period of runaway inflation, it was impossible to print enough banknotes to keep up with rising prices. Piles of notes ended up as worthless toys that children might play with.

Economic collapse

In 1919, Germany's economy was in peril. Industrial production was less than half of the 1913 level, the country had run up enormous debts during the war, and it also had to pay reparations to the Allies. In 1923, the economy collapsed under the strain and the German unit of currency, the mark, became worthless. Basic food items cost millions, even billions, of marks, and prices were so out of control that they could double in a day. Workers had to rush to buy their food as soon as they were paid before their wages lost all their value. Savings disappeared, and the middle class lost confidence in the economy. When French troops occupied the Ruhr to force reparation payments, the outlook became even bleaker. The mood of national despair was something the Nazis could exploit to their own advantage.

colors of the German imperial flag. It figured prominently on the banners and the armbands of party members.

The Nazi party whipped up support among the thousands of angry and disillusioned young men who roamed the streets of Munich. The storm troopers, or SA, were formed in October 1921 as the shock troops of the Nazis. They wore brown shirts and modeled themselves on the Freikorps. They were used to keep order at meetings. Hitler himself created a team of bodyguards—the SS, or Schutzstaffel ("protection squad"). These organizations gave the party an image of uniformed military

discipline. For instance, 6,000 storm troopers attended a parade in Munich in January 1923. As Germany reeled under the effects of the great inflation of 1923, such a display of order attracted support, particularly among the middle class, who now formed the majority of the party's members. Nazi membership totaled 55,000 in 1923.

A Failed Plot

Hitler's Nazi Party was growing in influence, but it was limited in its range. Its power did not extend outside Bavaria in the south of Germany. To achieve control of the whole country, Hitler would have to seize power in the capital, Berlin, hundreds of miles away. But, as recent events in Italy had shown, the idea was not out of the question. In Italy, fascist leader Benito Mussolini had created a movement, the

After the war, the Ruhr—an important industrial region—was occupied by French troops, shown here marching into a small German town in January 1923. German pride was hurt and the Nazis found it easy to exploit the national sense of shame and anger. They even circulated lurid horror stories of French brutality.

National Fascist Party, that was similar in aim to the Nazis. It ridiculed the weak Italian government and lamented Italy's postwar situation. Its troops were known as the blackshirts, and in October 1922 Mussolini ordered them

Heinrich Himmler (holding the flag) and storm troopers man a barricade by the Bavarian War Ministry as the Beer Hall Putsch of November 1923 is about to start.

to march on Rome, Italy's capital, to seize power on behalf of the nation. The Italian government, split by political infighting and fearing civil war, offered no opposition, and Mussolini seized the position of prime minister for himself.

Modeling himself on Mussolini, in November 1923 Hitler decided that he would seize the leading members of the Bavarian government (while they were speaking in a Munich beer hall)

and force them to march with him on Berlin. He persuaded one of the most distinguished generals of World War I, Erich Ludendorff, to join him.

The putsch, or plot to seize power, was a disaster. The Bavarian ministers were captured in the beer hall, but they escaped. When the storm troopers took to the streets of Munich, they were fired on and dispersed by the police. Hitler was wounded and arrested.

"The greatest mass orator of the age"

Opinions are divided about the reasons why Nazism took hold in Germany. Did the Weimar Republic fail to establish itself as a legitimate government with the German people, or were Hitler's unique gifts crucial to its success?

Journalist Konrad Heiden explains how Hitler sensed the needs of any crowd and how he promised to give them a voice:

"With unerring sureness, Hitler expressed the speechless panic of the masses faced by an invisible enemy and gave the nameless spectre a name. . . . His speeches are the daydreams of the soul of these masses. . . . They always begin with deep pessimism and end in overjoyed redemption, a triumphant, happy ending. . . . This makes him the greatest mass orator of the age."

Other historians have argued that the failure of the Weimar Republic to establish a strong democratic structure in Germany left the way open for the Nazis:

"After the First World War a strong government which had the entire population behind it was absent from German politics. Weimar governments lacked the basis of support and popular legitimacy to push through unpleasant but necessary measures democratically—a failure which led to the hyperinflation of 1922–1923. . . . The painful measures taken to introduce a stable currency rested on emergency measures which bypassed the Reichstag."

Historian Richard Bessel in Ian Kershaw (ed.), *Why Did Weimar Democracy Fail?* (Weidenfeld and Nicolson, 1990)

Hitler realized that his trial for treason would give him an ideal platform to proclaim the Nazi message. The proceedings would be reported across the nation. He protested that he had merely been fighting for Germany. He aroused a lot of public support and received a light sentence—five years in prison. He did not even have to serve that long because he was released within a year. Yet his campaign for power seemed to have stalled—in 1924, the Nazis gained only 3 percent of the vote in the Reichstag elections.

This picture shows Hitler looking out of the window of his cell in Landsberg prison, where he was imprisoned for less than a year in 1924. It was sold to Nazi supporters as a propaganda postcard. During his stay, he completed *Mein Kampf*, his autobiography.

CHAPTER 3

PROGRESS STALLS

Hitler's incarceration in prison in 1924 meant that the outlook for the Nazi Party was not promising. It was banned completely in Bavaria and, without strong leadership, it had been split by internal arguments. Yet Hitler remained confident. His belief that only he could be the savior of Germany had been reinforced during his prison sentence, and he planned ways to revive the Nazis' fortunes. In 1925, the ban on the party was lifted.

THE UNDISPUTED LEADER

Reluctantly, Hitler decided to put aside armed revolt in order to try to achieve power through the Reichstag elections. Small parties could win a few seats under the electoral voting system of the Weimar Constitution, but only a well-organized national party had a chance of success nationwide. Such a party would need one undisputed leader and a clear program that could be put into effect across Germany. Hitler identified a potential stumbling block: Gregor and Otto Strasser. He had entrusted these two brothers with the job of setting up party branches in Germany's northern industrial cities. If he could not control them, there was a risk that the Strassers would build their own power bases. Another rising Nazi, Joseph Goebbels, was proving to be almost as charismatic a public speaker as Hitler himself.

In 1926, Hitler made his move. Goebbels was won over by Hitler's powers of persuasion and he became one of his most trusted disciples. He was given control of the party in

The Hitler Youth was formed in 1926 in an effort to extend the appeal of the Nazi Party to the younger generation. There was a strong emphasis on uniforms, flags, and military-style marching.

A new policy

The failure of the Beer Hall Putsch convinced Hitler that the only path to power was through parliamentary elections:

"When I resume work it will be necessary to pursue a new policy. Instead of working to achieve power through an armed coup, we shall have to hold our noses and enter the Reichstag against the Catholic and communist deputies. If out-voting them takes longer than out-shooting them, at least the result will be guaranteed by the Weimar Constitution. Any lawful process is slow. . . . Sooner or later we will have a majority . . . and after that . . . Germany."

K. Luedecke, *I Knew Hitler* (E. Scribner's Sons, 1938)

Berlin, and at once proved himself to be a brilliant and unscrupulous propagandist. He instinctively knew how to spread damaging lies about his opponents that would be believed by the general public. He also ruthlessly used the local storm troopers to beat up and intimidate enemies, all in the name of keeping order. Gregor Strasser was also confronted and told directly by Hitler that many of his policies were ridiculous. He was forced to accept Hitler's leadership.

THE PARTY GROWS STRONGER

The next step was to establish an

Hitler surrounded by an admiring group of Hitler Youth members and storm troopers at the SA headquarters in Munich. Swastika armbands were a compulsory part of the Nazi uniform.

TURNING POINTS IN HISTORY

Oaths of loyalty

One of the dangers that faced a growing Nazi Party in 1925 and 1926 was internal division. It could have split into a lot of smaller parties run by local leaders unprepared to accept Hitler's leadership. Some Nazis already complained that Hitler was not even a proper German, but an Austrian. Hitler responded by intimidating his rivals and bribing them with senior posts if they would accept his leadership totally. At a party rally in July 1926, the storm troopers were made to swear oaths of loyalty to the leader as they marched past him, with their right hands stretched out toward him in what became a compulsory salute. Any further threats to Hitler's leadership evaporated. Some Nazis even began to revere him as a kind of god.

efficient national organization. Party headquarters were set up in each of Germany's thirty-five electoral regions to give the Nazis a strong base on which to contest elections. These were linked to local branches. Local leaders could aspire to positions of influence as long as they swore their allegiance to Hitler. Hitler, in fact, encouraged young Nazis to struggle for control of their local parties, as it went along with his belief that life was a continual struggle in which only the fittest would survive. The party began to attract many able and well-educated young men. In fact, more than 90 percent of the members of the Nazi Party were male: The Nazi creed was that a woman's place was in the home.

Hitler believed fervently that the future of Nazi Germany lay in its children, and he felt that the party should have as much influence as schools on their education. To attract young supporters and to build a power base from which future storm troopers could be recruited, the Hitler Youth movement was founded in 1926. Boys and girls were organized but treated differently: The boys' section prepared members for military service, the girls' to be good German mothers.

As a result of its growth into a party with truly national reach, the Nazis began to enlist the support of groups of voters that it had never previously attracted. One such group

The Depression affected the lives of poor German farmers, such as these women gathering the asparagus crop. The Nazis courted their support by promising to respect the relationship between farmers and the German land.

was the peasant farmers of northern Germany. Falling prices following the hyperinflation of 1923 had bankrupted many farmers. The Nazis flattered the farmers that their honest labor on the land made them the heart of Germany; there was much talk of German "blood and soil," and promises of help if the Nazis came to power. By 1928, the Nazis were attracting nearly 20 percent of the votes in some rural areas at a time when voters in the big cities virtually ignored them.

Signs of Recovery

The Nazi Party grew most rapidly when it could exploit the fears and insecurities of the German people. When times were bad and the economy was failing, Germans responded to the Nazis' message, outlined in 1921 in a program

Hitler sought to forge links with other political groups that might support the Nazi program. Here he is shown in August 1927 meeting leaders of the National People's Party, who were sympathetic to many of his aims.

of twenty-five points, to overturn the Treaty of Versailles, revive Germany through a policy of expansion to the east, and strip the Jews of their civil rights.

However, in the late 1920s, the situation in Germany began to improve. After 1924, the economy stabilized and then began to grow. New investment began to pour in, especially from the United States, and an energetic foreign minister (and ardent nationalist), Gustav Stresemann, strove to repair Germany's relations with its old enemies. He realized that the harshness of Versailles could be softened by

Gustav Stresemann was a German politician and statesman who served as chancellor and as foreign minister during the Weimar Republic. He was Germany's most successful politician of the 1920s. He managed to win back the trust of Germany's old enemies and renegotiate the war reparation payments. He died in 1929 at the age of 51.

conservative National People's Party 14 percent. The votes cast for them at this election secured a mere twelve Nazi deputies in the Reichstag. Joseph Goebbels and Gregor Strasser were among them.

OTHER IMPORTANT VOICES

Two men who were to have immense influence on the development of the Nazi Party were now active in the movement. One was Hermann Göring, a World War I air ace with aristocratic connections. Göring saw himself as a war hero who brought glamor to the party. His association gave Nazism a superficial gloss of respectability. He had been involved with the Nazis in the early 1920s as the head of the storm troopers. He had left Germany after the failure of the Beer Hall Putsch, but Hitler had persuaded him to run for election, and he was one of the twelve deputies elected in 1928. Intensely loyal to Hitler, he was now one of the most important figures in the party.

Heinrich Himmler was the other influential figure. Though not a born leader, Himmler was conscientious, hardworking, and ambitious. However, he also had a passionate hatred of the Jews and was obsessed with the superiority and purity of the German race. Hitler installed him as head of his bodyguard unit, the SS. Himmler dressed this unit

careful diplomacy. He managed to negotiate a reduction in the total reparations bill, and got an agreement that payments could now be stretched over sixty years, rather than thirty as had been originally demanded.

As the future of Germany appeared brighter, the fortunes of the Nazis dwindled correspondingly. In the elections of 1928, they won only 2.6 percent of the votes, fewer even than in 1924. The Social Democratic Party gained nearly 30 percent and the

The mood in Germany

Ian Kershaw is one of many historians who point out that Germany was quite stable between 1924 and 1929. As he puts it:

"These were Weimar's 'golden years.' . . . In the economy, industrial production came to surpass the pre-war level for the first time. Real wages did the same. The welfare state made impressive progress. Health provision was far superior to the prewar period. Public spending on housing increased massively. . . . The first glimmers of a mass-consumer society were visible."

However, the mood on the streets was much more volatile. An English writer, Christopher Isherwood, records his own memories of Berlin in the 1920s:

"Berlin was in a state of civil war. Hate exploded suddenly, without warning, out of nowhere; at street corners, in restaurants, cinemas, dance halls, swimming baths; at midnight, after breakfast, in the middle of the afternoon. Knives were whipped out, blows were dealt with spiked rings, beer mugs, chair-legs or leaded clubs, bullets slashed the advertisements on the poster columns."

Ian Kershaw, *Hitler: 1889–1936, Hubris* (Allen Lane, Penguin, 1998); Christopher Isherwood, *The Berlin Stories* (New Directions Publishing Corporation, 1954)

The son of a schoolmaster, Heinrich Himmler (1900–1945) had the appearance and manner of a dull pen-pusher. However, Hitler admired his fanatical anti-Semitism and made him the first head of the notorious SS.

in a black uniform to distinguish it from the brown-shirted storm troopers, and enforced strict discipline. The SS became the party's secret police, always on the lookout for threats to Hitler's position and, when ordered to do so, to deal with them brutally.

CHAPTER 4

SEIZING CONTROL

A shattering blow struck the world economy in 1929. After the boom years of the 1920s, the New York Stock Exchange went into freefall in October as confidence in the U.S. economy evaporated. The revival of Germany's finances had been based on short-term loans from U.S. banks, but now these loans were called in. The German economy collapsed—industrial production fell by 40 percent in three years, and unemployment soared.

A FAILING DEMOCRACY

To add to Germany's problems, its skillful foreign minister, Stresemann, died in October. The Weimar government proved powerless to deal with the economic crisis. In 1930, Heinrich Brüning became the new first minister or chancellor. His Catholic Center Party had gained only just over 12 percent of the votes in the 1928 elections, so Brüning tried to govern through forming a coalition with other parties. This plan backfired, and the parliamentary sessions became so unruly that the Reichstag set a limit on the number of times that it would meet. Before 1930, it had been in session for an average of some 100 days a year. Between October 1930 and March 1931, the figure was only 50 days, and then only 24 days between April 1931 and June 1932. Between July 1932 and February 1933, it met for only 3

This table shows how the Nazis went from zero support in 1920 to being the largest political party in Germany in 1933. The refusal of the Communists and Social Democrats to work together to oppose the Nazis meant that Hitler could easily outmaneuver them after 1933.

VOTING PATTERNS IN THE WEIMAR REPUBLIC							
Parties	Percentage of total votes cast in elections						
	1920 June	1924 Dec.	1928 May	1930 Sept.	1932 July	1932 Nov.	1933 March
Communist	2.1	9.0	10.6	13.1	14.5	16.9	12.3
Social Democratic	21.7	26.0	29.8	24.5	21.6	20.4	18.3
Center	13.6	13.6	12.1	11.8	12.5	11.9	11.2
National People's	15.1	20.5	14.2	7.0	6.2	8.9	8.0
Nazis	–	3.0	2.6	18.3	37.4	33.1	43.9

In July 1931, the Berlin Stock Exchange (pictured) was temporarily closed to avoid panic selling. It was an obvious sign of the crippled state of the German economy.

days. Democracy was replaced by rule by decrees issued by the president, Hindenburg, the distinguished World War I military leader.

Taking the Opportunity

Hitler saw an opportunity to exploit the collapse of the economy and the failure of parliamentary government. Lingering discontents and humiliating memories had been revived in Germany by the misery of the Depression, and his small but well-organized party was well-placed to take advantage. Hitler had one overriding aim which he was prepared to achieve at any cost—power. He began to make more public speeches and to tailor them to specific audiences.

Hitler excelled at telling different audiences something that each wanted to hear. For example, he would promise farmers higher prices for their grain, and then in a speech the following day pledge cheaper bread for the workers. Sixty percent of the Nazi voters were middle class, and Hitler enticed them with visions of a rejuvenated economy, new job opportunities, the suppression of Communism, and a return to traditional German values of hard work and sober living. The Communists were a particular target. He argued that they were more than a threat to the middle class—he claimed that they were under the control of a foreign power, the Soviet Union.

Election Success

Hitler now worked on broadening his popular appeal. He still enjoyed strong support among the farmers who had been battered by falling world prices, but now he also reached out

This huge parade through the streets of Nuremberg shows how the Nazis used massed ranks of marchers and dramatic banners to create an impact.

to businessmen. They would be more likely to see him in a sober business suit than a Nazi uniform, but the promises remained the same: Suppression of the rebellious workers and a more stable economy. In return, they opened their wallets to help finance a party that appeared to be their savior.

To bolster feelings of national unity, the Nazis sought to attach blame to common enemies. At home, the Communists and Jews were presented as the main threats. Abroad, it was those who had humiliated Germany at Versailles. The Slav peoples of Eastern Europe, who had emerged from the collapse of the Russian and Austrian empires after World War I, were also targeted. The Nazis argued that they should be absorbed into a greater Germany.

The results of the elections of September 1930 gave dramatic proof of the success of Hitler's methods. The Nazis won over 18 percent of the votes. They were now the second-largest party after the Social Democrats, but the Social Democratic Party was a toothless opposition. Its core support, the workers, were demoralized by unemployment, and the party was being challenged by the Communist Party, which preached violent revolution. The Communists got stronger in every election between 1920 and 1932, giving Hitler more and more reason to portray them as a serious threat to Germany.

THE NUREMBERG RALLIES

A public image of disciplined power was vital if the Nazis wanted to take advantage of the unrest brought about by the breakdown of German society during the Depression. Every year, starting in 1927, the ancient city of Nuremberg became the stage for a huge display—the Nuremberg Rally. This was a perfect setting in which the traditional values of the old Germany could be imaginatively linked with the new Germany that the Nazis held up as their dream.

With each year that passed, the rallies became more awe-inspiring and elaborate. Well over 100,000 party members might be packed onto the parade ground, many in uniform and backed by row upon row of banners bearing swastikas. Dominating the arena was a huge platform—Hitler would make his way along the central avenue to the solemn tone of a funeral march. In later rallies, rows of searchlights would pierce the sky above the crowd,

VOICES FROM HISTORY

Not what he seemed

Despite the cruelty of its underlying beliefs, Nazism could assume a respectable face in public. A member of Hitler's inner circle, architect Albert Speer, gives an example:

"What was decisive for me was a speech by Hitler which my students finally persuaded me to attend. From what I had read in the opposition press, I expected to find a screaming, gesticulating fanatic in uniform, instead of which we were confronted with a quiet man in a dark suit who addressed us in the measured tones of an academic."

A letter written in 1953 by Speer to his daughter, quoted in Gitta Sereny, *Albert Speer: His Battle with Truth* (Macmillan, 1995)

Violence between opposing political groups, particularly Nazis and Communists, often erupted on the streets of Germany in the early 1930s. Here, a casualty is being carried away on a stretcher. The boy in the background is carrying what appears to be an election poster supporting Hitler.

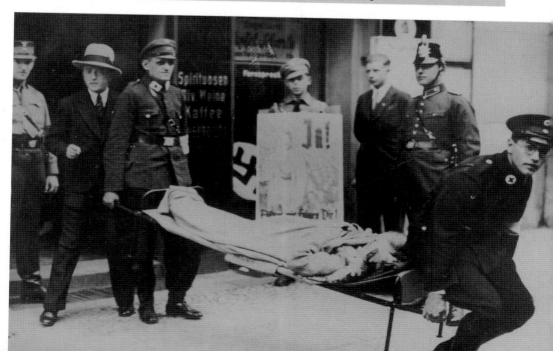

Horst Wessel (1907–1930) was a Nazi SA member who was shot and killed in Berlin in a dispute with some Communists. Goebbels seized the chance to turn him into a martyr, holding a public funeral.

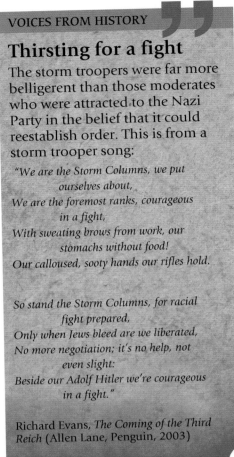

VOICES FROM HISTORY

Thirsting for a fight

The storm troopers were far more belligerent than those moderates who were attracted to the Nazi Party in the belief that it could reestablish order. This is from a storm trooper song:

"We are the Storm Columns, we put ourselves about,
We are the foremost ranks, courageous in a fight,
With sweating brows from work, our stomachs without food!
Our calloused, sooty hands our rifles hold.

So stand the Storm Columns, for racial fight prepared,
Only when Jews bleed are we liberated,
No more negotiation; it's no help, not even slight:
Beside our Adolf Hitler we're courageous in a fight."

Richard Evans, *The Coming of the Third Reich* (Allen Lane, Penguin, 2003)

who were saluting ecstatically and shouting "Heil Hitler." Then Hitler would start to address the masses. He was a master of his craft. He would start slowly, gradually building up in an overwhelmingly emotional crescendo: "Is there anything left in Germany they [the Jews] haven't ruined?" was one impassioned climax.

The storm troopers adopted a disciplined manner at Hitler's rallies, but they would reveal a very different face out on the streets of Germany's big cities. There, violent hatred of their rivals—above all the Communists—was the order of the day. Their propaganda, however, carefully glossed over the reality. For example, when one party member, Horst Wessel, was shot in Berlin by Communists after a private dispute over a girl, he was hailed as a Nazi martyr and his song, "The Flag's Held High," was turned into the Nazi anthem by Goebbels.

TURNING POINTS IN HISTORY

Hard times

Every social class had reason to lament the Depression of 1929 to 1932, and this is why it was such a significant turning point for Germany.

Industrial workers suffered, as did middle-class people who lost money when the banks collapsed. In rural areas, farmers suffered because prices were low and agricultural workers were thrown off large estates.

The passion and patriotism of the Nazis was attractive in such desperate times.

This Nazi poster for the presidential election of 1932 depicts a heroic-looking German working man staring out over the slogan "We want work and bread! Vote for Hitler!"

MORE ELECTION GAINS

The presidential elections of March 1932 provided dramatic proof of the power of Nazi propaganda. Hitler (who by now had become a German citizen) decided to run against Hindenburg, now an old man of eighty-four. Hitler lost but, drawing heavily on the discontent of a nation demoralized by the Depression, he captured a staggering 13 million votes. Four months later, in the Reichstag elections, the Nazis wielded every campaigning trick in their armory. Posters appeared everywhere, patriotic music blared from loudspeakers, storm troopers paraded through the streets, and Hitler visited all parts of the country. The Nazis promised to solve the economic crisis, although the practical details weren't made clear.

The campaign was a huge success. The Nazi vote doubled to 37.4 percent. The Nazis were now the largest elected party, with 100 more seats than their nearest rivals, the Social Democrats. Hitler's bandwagon appeared to be unstoppable, and he had a new demand: Hindenburg must appoint him as chancellor.

Hindenburg, however, had other ideas. He had little personal sympathy for the upstart Hitler, and he chose instead to ally himself with his own choice for chancellor, Franz von Papen, a Catholic aristocrat. Von Papen's

WHY DID IT HAPPEN

The seeds of success

Historian Klaus Fischer thinks that the economic conditions of the time laid the foundations for the Nazis' success:

"The Nazi upsurge can be attributed primarily to the Depression that had ruined many German businesses and led to a tragic increase in unemployment. The Depression, in turn, stirred up a pervasive fear of impending political chaos, leading to an acute crisis in confidence for the democratic system. . . . The Nazis were undoubtedly beneficiaries of popular antidemocratic feelings that they themselves did not create."

For his part, historian Wolfram Pyta argues that the Nazis gained popularity because they were able to tap into the mood of demoralized German voters:

"The Nazi programme was skillfully tailored to winning the rural vote. It created a conservative image for itself by speaking up for the preservation of the rural way of life . . . it invoked the idea of a 'People's Community' transcending the classes which awoke a multitude of hopes, particularly among parish priests and teachers who felt they were being taken seriously. . . . The Nazis were the only party able to present an attractive offering to all village authorities."

Klaus Fischer, *Nazi Germany* (Constable, 1995); Wolfram Pyta quoted in Neil Gregor (ed.), *Nazism* (Oxford University Press, 2000)

On January 30, 1933, Adolf Hitler, the son of a minor official from Austria, was formally confirmed as chancellor of Germany by President Hindenburg. Few realized just how quickly Hitler and his Nazi Party would take absolute control of the country.

policy was to bypass parliamentary government altogether and rule through decree. This policy had little public support, but Hitler also had problems to overcome. Economic conditions in Germany were at last improving, and people were beginning to blame the Nazi Party for causing violence. More elections were held in November, and the Nazis actually lost 2 million votes. On top of this, their electioneering efforts were draining their party's finances.

By late 1932, political turmoil engulfed the German political system. In parliament, the Communists and the Nazis were locked in constant confrontation. Von Papen had no effective support and he resigned as chancellor in December. An army general, Kurt von Schleicher, took over. His solution was to suppress the Nazis and declare a military government. Von Papen, angry at losing his office, could see a way to get back into power. He would ask Hindenburg to make Hitler chancellor. Von Papen thought that he could control the Nazis by using his own supporters to box Hitler in. On January 30, 1933, Hitler was finally appointed chancellor. But if von Papen now thought that he had Hitler in his power, he was mistaken.

CHAPTER 5

THE ROAD TO POWER

On the night of January 30, 1933, when Hitler was appointed chancellor, Joseph Goebbels, the head of the party in Berlin, organized a vast parade to march through the city. It was meant to convince voters that this was an extraordinary national development. But politically, Hitler's position looked weak. It seemed at first as if the Nazis might successfully be held in check as von Papen had hoped. Hitler was part of a coalition government and only two other Nazis were appointed ministers.

However, one of them, Wilhelm Frick, was minister of the interior and the other, Göring, was made head of the police of Germany's largest state, Prussia. Law and order in Germany was under their control. Almost immediately they started to draw up plans to ban the Communist Party.

While political opposition to Hitler was fragmented, it was possible that the army might rise against him. Hitler's own military career had been undistinguished—he had not risen

Hitler with members of his first cabinet in January 1933. Only two other cabinet members were Nazis. They were Hermann Göring, sitting on Hitler's right, and Wilhelm Frick, shown directly behind Hitler.

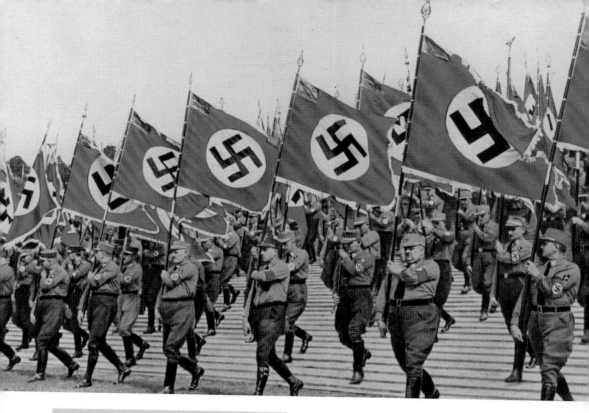

A public display of power, this parade of Nazi Party officials was held in Nuremberg in 1933, the year that Hitler became chancellor. It reveals how dominant a symbol the swastika had become. It is not only the central emblem of every flag, but is also worn on the armband of each flagbearer.

higher than corporal—and he knew that many officers looked down on him. He acted quickly to stifle any challenge. On February 3, he met army leaders to promise that he would dismantle the Treaty of Versailles and rebuild the army. He even outlined a new military strategy—the invasion of Eastern Europe to establish a greater Germany in which the native Slavs would be replaced by German settlers. This vision appealed to the army high command, and they confirmed that they would not intervene if Hitler moved to consolidate his power.

Horror and joy

Some of the mixed emotions aroused by Nazism are evident in this eyewitness account by a teenage girl, Melita Maschman, of an event on January 30, 1933 :

"For hours the columns marched by . . . At one point somebody suddenly leapt from the ranks of the marchers and struck a man who had been standing only a few paces away from us, perhaps he had made a hostile remark. I saw him fall to the ground with blood streaming down his face and I heard him cry out . . .

"The horror it inspired in me was almost imperceptibly spiced with an intoxicating joy . . . I was overcome with a burning desire to belong to these people for whom it was a matter of life and death."

Richard Evans, *The Coming of the Third Reich* (Allen Lane, Penguin, 2003)

Documents and papers raided from Communist offices are loaded onto a truck to be taken away and destroyed. Once Hitler became chancellor, political opponents were systematically suppressed until the Nazi Party had complete control over the tools of power in Germany.

UNLAWFUL PRACTICES

Hitler's next move was to announce another election to be held on March 5. The police, now under Nazi control, were used to intimidate and attack the Nazis' opponents. Communists were declared enemies of Germany by the Nazi propaganda machine. Communist supporters were to be destroyed.

Newspapers supporting the Center Party were closed down. Businessmen were told they must contribute to the Nazi election fund if they wanted the police to suppress strikes. Communist and Social Democratic demonstrations were broken up and their party offices were vandalized. In Prussia, the police were told by Göring to ignore Nazi violence: "Every bullet that now leaves the mouth of a police pistol is my bullet. If you call that murder, then I am the murderer, for I gave the order

From the boycott to the Holocaust

Hatred of the Jews was central to Nazi ideology. Storm troopers openly poured out anti-Semitic abuse in their marching songs. Soon after the Nazis came to power at the end of March 1933, they announced a boycott of all Jewish businesses. Every Jewish shop across Germany was closed on April 1. Storm troopers stood on guard outside to make sure that no one broke the ban. "An imposing spectacle . . . a huge moral victory for Germany: we have shown everyone abroad that we can call on the whole nation for action," wrote Goebbels in his diary. This was the first step on a long and bitter road that led eventually to the stripping of citizenship from Jews and ultimately to the extermination programs of the Holocaust.

"No Mercy Now"

The next turn of events proved an extraordinary slice of good fortune for the Nazis. A young Dutchman, Marinus van der Lubbe, decided to launch a one-man protest against Nazi brutality. On February 27, he broke into the Reichstag building and set it on fire. Hitler, Göring, and Goebbels rushed to

and stand by it."

Many Communists looked on with divided feelings. Their political advisers in the Soviet Union thought that the violence of the Nazis might actually bring about the workers' revolution that they craved. They were prepared to wait.

The Reichstag building in Berlin goes up in flames on February 27, 1933. The Nazis seized the opportunity to pin the blame for the fire on the Communists.

Election leaflets litter the sidewalks of Berlin in the days before the elections of March 1933. These were to be the last free elections in Germany until the end of World War II. Despite their tactics of violence and intimidation, the Nazis failed to gain a full majority, but soon afterward they enforced their rule by dictatorship.

the scene of the blaze in Berlin that night. Hitler stared at the sea of flames and then burst out to his colleagues: "There will be no more mercy now; anyone who stands in our way will be butchered. The German people will no longer understand leniency. Every Communist functionary will be shot where he is found. The Communist deputies must be hanged this very night. Everybody in league with the Communists is to be arrested. Against Social Democrats too there will be no mercy!"

The Communists were the immediate target. Four thousand leading figures were rounded up and many were dispatched to the first concentration camps. A law was enacted that gave Hitler's government the power to limit freedom of speech and the right to hold meetings, and permission to search houses and read private mail. Freedoms and individual rights once guaranteed by the Weimar Constitution were overturned. Hindenburg, who also viewed the Communist workers' movement with suspicion, was persuaded to sign the law.

Despite this background of massive coercion, the Nazis only won 43.9 percent of the votes in the election of

March 5. However, with the addition of another 8 percent from the National People's Party, which agreed to support the Nazis, they did have a small parliamentary majority. The Communists and Social Democrats still attracted 30 percent of the votes in the face of all the negative propaganda directed at them. The new Reichstag was scheduled to meet for the first time on March 21. Now Germany would see how the Nazis intended to exert their power.

A line of electors line up to cast their votes on the day of the Reichstag elections in March 1933. The only election poster on display depicts Hitler alongside Hindenburg, as if he had the president's sole support. Its slogan declared "The Reich will never be destroyed if you are united and loyal."

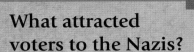

What attracted voters to the Nazis?

What was the catalyst that caused German electors to vote for Nazi rule? One historian suggests that, in one town at least, the vigor of the local Nazis was crucial to winning over local support:

"Thalburg's Nazis created their own image by their own initiative, vigour and propaganda. They knew exactly what needed to be done to effect the transfer of power to themselves in the spring of 1933. . . . Hitler, Goebbels, and the other Nazi leaders provided the political decisions, ideology, national propaganda and, later, the control over the government which made the revolution possible. But it was in the hundreds of localities like Thalburg all over Germany that the revolution was made actual. They formed the foundation of the Third Reich."

Others think that the anticommunist feelings of Germans who were not otherwise Nazis were exploited by Hitler:

"The long-standing hatred of Socialism and Communism was played upon by Nazi propaganda and turned into outright anti-Communist paranoia. Pumped up by the Nazis, fear of a communist uprising was in the air. The closer the election came, the shriller grew the hysteria. The full-scale assault on the left was, therefore, sure of massive popular support."

William Sheridan Allen, *The Nazi Seizure of Power: The Experience of a Single Town* (Eyre and Spottiswood, 1966); Ian Kershaw, *Hitler:1889–1936, Hubris* (Allen Lane, Penguin, 1998)

CHAPTER 6

THE NAZI TYRANNY

The newly elected Reichstag met for the first time on March 21, the first day of spring. To reflect their links with Germany's sacred traditions, the Nazis organized a service at one of Berlin's most important churches, the Potsdam Garrison Church, where the Prussian kings lay buried. The impression they wanted to give was that they reached back in an unbroken line to the great German war heroes of the past, such as Frederick the Great.

TOTAL CONTROL

The display of pomp and dignity on March 21 soon gave way to a very different reality. The first session of the new parliament was held in the Kroll Opera House, as the Reichstag was in ruins. It soon became brutally clear who was in charge. Most of the eighty-one elected Communist deputies had either been arrested or were prevented from attending. Storm troopers and the SS were everywhere, even guarding the doors of the building once they had been shut when the session began. Huge banners bearing the swastika hung from the walls. For the Nazis the swastika, an ancient symbol representing life and good luck, became the badge of Aryan power. In Nazi ideology, Aryan stood for white, non-Jewish, and racially superior.

Hitler's first move was to ask the Reichstag to pass a law, to be known as the Enabling Act, that would give him full control over government for four years. Few voices were raised in dissent. The National People's Party, which had seen its voters swing behind the Nazis

Many observers had no illusions about Hitler. In this poster from the United States published around 1934, he is shown as a gorilla clutching a defenseless maiden, Germany. In his hand is a boulder labeled "tolerance."

"The new German kingdom"

In February 1933, Hitler asked the German people to give him four years in which to prove himself:

"For 14 years [i.e., 1919–1933] the parties of disintegration, of the November Revolution, have seduced and abused the German people. For fourteen years they wreaked destruction, infiltration and dissolution. Considering this it is not presumptuous of me to stand before the nation today, and plead to it: German people give us four years and then pass judgement upon us, German people give us four years, and I swear to you, just as we, just as I have taken office, so shall I leave it. . . . I cherish the firm conviction that the hour will come at last in which the millions who despise us today will stand by us and with us will hail the new, hard-won and painfully acquired German Reich we have created together, the new German kingdom of greatness and power and glory and justice. Amen."

Quoted in Richard Evans, *The Coming of the Third Reich* (Allen Lane, Penguin, 2003)

The left-wing writer, publisher, and pacifist Carl von Ossietzky was among the many dissidents sent to concentration camps. He was arrested for "revealing state secrets" in 1933.

in recent elections, supported it. The Catholic Center Party, in exchange for some insignificant concessions, also voted in favor. Only the Social Democrats held out against the measure, their leader Otto Wels evoking the principles of humanity, justice, and freedom.

Hitler's reasonable manner suddenly changed and he tore into the Social Democrats with savage contempt: "Germany will be free, but not through you," he shouted to the cheers of the Nazi deputies. The vote was then taken. Four hundred and forty-one deputies voted in favor, and ninety-four—the Social Democrats—against. The Enabling Act was in force the very next day. This was the moment when democracy disappeared under the Nazi tyranny. The voice of the people expressed through parliament was silenced.

CONCENTRATION CAMPS

The powers of the Enabling Act meant that Hitler could now extend the iron grip of Nazism over Germany. The first concentration camps had been set up in March 1933, and soon Communists and other political opponents of the

The burning of books became a familiar public event in Nazi Germany. Texts by famous Jews and Communists were targeted. In this picture from May 1933, Nazi officials and civilians in the crowd give the Nazi salute over the smoldering ashes.

Nazis were summarily imprisoned in them. Violence against the Jews was unleashed at street level. Systematic persecution, exclusion from public life, and eventual extermination followed inexorably.

Any organization that was deemed a threat to Nazi interests was targeted. The trade unions felt the first blow. On May 1, the Nazis announced a workers' public holiday: a "Day of National Labor." A million workers, many of whom had opposed the Nazi rise to power, gathered at a huge rally outside Berlin which was addressed by Hitler himself surrounded by supporters waving Nazi banners. The very next

VOICES FROM HISTORY

A champion of freedom

The only politician to speak against Hitler's Enabling Act was the leader of the Social Democratic Party, Otto Wels:

"We the German Social Democratic Party pledge ourselves solemnly in this historic hour to the principles of humanity and justice, of freedom and socialism. No enabling act can give you the power to destroy ideas which are eternal and indestructible."

William L. Shirer, *The Rise and Fall of the Third Reich* (Secker & Warburg, 1960)

A watershed moment

Hitler's power over Germany became virtually absolute when the Enabling Act became law on March 23. The Reichstag became little more than a public stage from which Hitler could address the assembled Nazi deputies. By the summer of 1933, all the other political parties had been banned, destroyed, or forced to accept the dominance of the Nazis. An undercurrent of terror ran through German life because the Nazis were prepared to use their unrestricted power without any regard for human rights or civil liberties. Communists and Jews were to be the focus of the regime's hate campaign.

day, all German trade union offices were raided. Free unions were outlawed and members found themselves under the control of the German Labor Front, which was a newly created Nazi version of a trade union.

Next, the Nazis ruthlessly stamped out political opposition. The Communists had already been banned, but worse was to come. On June 21, the interior minister, Wilhelm Frick, ordered the banning of the Social Democratic Party throughout Germany. "The Social Democratic party has been dissolved. The total state won't have to wait for long now," wrote Goebbels in his diary. The Center Party posed a more difficult problem because of its strong connections with the Catholic Church. The Nazis, however, argued that its campaign against Communism and atheism would benefit the church, and so the party also accepted Nazi rule. It even agreed under von Papen's guidance to dissolve itself on July 5, 1933. The smaller political parties were soon bullied into submission, and the regional governments of the individual German states were also dissolved.

ECONOMIC IMPROVEMENTS

The impact of this new regime of repression was partly offset by a revival in the economy. Hitler had little time for economics, and he was confident that his long-term strategy of expansion to the east would open up new resources of land that would allow Germany to become self-sufficient. However, he did manage to reinvigorate the employment market through two major new programs.

The first initiative was rearmament, or the buildup of weapons. This move was a closely guarded secret shared only with the army because it was a direct violation of the Treaty of Versailles. Hitler did not want to arouse the suspicions of France and Britain at this stage. The second was a program of construction of housing and roads, of which the Autobahnen—the freeways—got most attention in the press. The autobahns did more than provide new jobs; they seemed a concrete representation of the new modern Germany that Hitler had promised. The Depression was coming to an end, in Europe at least, and Germany was

The opening in May 1935 of the first Autobahn, or freeway, from Munich to the Austrian border was an ideal opportunity for the Nazi propaganda machine to sing the praises of the new regime. It polished up the image of the Nazis as masters of new technologies and engineering.

experiencing a new sense of economic optimism. Many were prepared to applaud the Nazi regime for this and turn a blind eye to its brutalities.

Night of the Long Knives

The storm troopers, under their leader Ernst Röhm, considered that they were part of Hitler's inner circle. They expected that he would offer them the most important jobs and perhaps even a central role in a new German army. Hitler, however, knew that to administer Germany effectively and embark on a rearmament program, he would need the support of the existing army and state civil service. The storm troopers were not part of these plans. Another threat to the SA also materialized when Göring created a new Nazi police force, the Gestapo. Leading storm troopers began to talk of engineering a "second revolution" to put them back at the center of power.

Relations between the party leaders and the storm troopers remained strained for several months. Finally, Hitler was persuaded to snuff out any threat from Röhm and his allies. On the "Night of the Long Knives," June 30, 1934, the SS with army support killed Röhm and about 100 others. An emotional Hitler informed the Reichstag that he had been forced to act as judge and jury to safeguard the security of the German people. The storm troopers were subdued while the SS and the Gestapo tightened their control over the party and its enemies.

On August 2, 1934, President Hindenburg died at the age of eighty-six. He had already been effectively elbowed aside by the Nazis, and Hitler now formally took over all his executive powers. The German army was forced to swear unconditional allegiance to "Adolf Hitler, the führer [leader] of the German nation and people." Hitler's seizure of power was complete.

The body of Paul von Hindenburg on his deathbed in August 1934. Following Hindenburg's death, Hitler merged the presidency with the office of chancellor under the title of leader and chancellor (Führer und Reichskanzler).

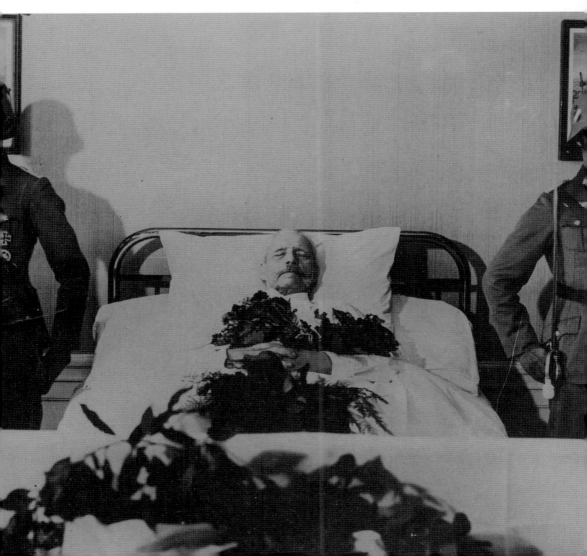

RESTORING NATIONAL PRIDE

The reasons for Hitler's success can be summarized: The fear of the Communists, which enabled him to suppress human rights supposedly for the good of the German people; the fanatical enthusiasm of his followers; and the lack of opposition to what was happening. Too many Germans turned a blind eye to the terror and intimidation, partly out of fear but partly because they wanted to believe in the great program of change and renewal that Hitler promised. After Germany's postwar humiliations, it was all too easy to accept the arguments of a man who promised to restore the nation's pride.

The unfolding horror of Nazi dictatorship could not be concealed, even though investment in building new roads and armaments led to more employment and a reviving economy. Historian Richard Evans sums up what was still to come in his book, *The Coming of the Third Reich*: "Now [with full control of Germany] the Nazis would set about constructing a racial utopia, in which a purebred nation of heroes would prepare as rapidly and as thoroughly as possible for the ultimate test of German racial superiority: a war in which they would crush their enemies and establish a new European order that would eventually come to dominate the world."

(Opposite) As Hitler's grip on power grew tighter, Nazi rallies became increasingly grandiose and preoccupied with rituals that had an almost religious dimension. Shown here, at a 1934 rally, is the blessing of the flags.

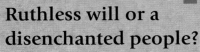

WHY DID IT HAPPEN

Ruthless will or a disenchanted people?

The underlying reasons for the overwhelming success of the Nazi party are hard to pin down with certainty. Some historians, like William Carr, stress the dynamism and passion of the Nazis:

"What was compelling about Hitler and what distinguished his party from other right-wing parties were not only the external trappings—the feverish activity, the endless marching, the mass rallies, and the ceaseless propaganda drives—important though these were in gathering votes, but above all the ruthless will to victory and fanatical sense of commitment emanating from the führer and his followers."

Others, including the left-wing historian Eric Hobsbawm, think that Germany's situation after World War I was to blame:

"The best conditions for the triumph of the crazy ultra-Right were an old state and its ruling mechanism which could no longer function; a mass of disenchanted, disorientated and discontented citizens who no longer knew where their loyalties lay; strong socialist movements threatening or appearing to threaten social revolution, but not actually in a position to achieve it; and a move of national resentment against the peace treaties of 1918–1920."

William Carr, *Hitler, A Study in Personality and Politics* (Edward Arnold, 1978); Eric Hobsbawm, *Age of Extremes: The Short Twentieth Century, 1914–1991* (Michael Joseph, 1994)

THE RISE OF NAZISM TIMELINE

1889
April 20: Hitler born in Braunau in Austria

1914 Outbreak of World War I. Hitler joins the German army

1918 Germany suffers defeat in war. Unrest in major German cities .

1919
June: Treaty of Versailles brings humiliation on Germany
July: Friedrich Ebert establishes the Weimar Constitution
September: Hitler attends a meeting of the German Workers' Party in Munich. He joins and soon builds a reputation as an orator

1920
February: The German Workers' Party is renamed the German National Socialist Workers' Party

1921
July: Hitler establishes himself as leader of the Nazis

1923
July: Inflation hits Germany and leads to major recruitment to the Nazi Party and its storm troopers

November: Hitler launches the Beer Hall Putsch in Munich. It fails and Hitler is arrested

1924 Hitler serves time in prison for his part in the putsch. He writes *Mein Kampf* while in custody

1925–6 Hitler re-establishes his leadership of the Nazis and starts creating a nationwide party. Greater economic stability in Germany hampers the party's growth

1928 Elections reveal the continuing weakness of the party. It achieves only 2.6 percent of the votes, and 12 seats in the Reichstag

1929 The stock market crash in New York causes U.S. loans to be withdrawn from Germany. Start of a major economic depression

1930 The Nazis win 18.3 percent of the vote in the elections and 107 seats

1932
April: Hitler runs against Hindenburg in the presidential election, loses, but gets 13 million votes

July: Elections make the Nazis the largest party in the Reichstag with 230 seats
November: New elections. The Nazis lose ground

1933
January: Hitler is made chancellor in an attempt to box him in within a conservative government
February: Hitler orders new elections, and uses the Reichstag fire to justify human rights restrictions and anticommunism
March: In the elections, the Nazis win 43.9 percent of the votes. Hitler forces through an Enabling Act giving him absolute power
April: A boycott of Jewish businesses is enforced
July: All political parties dissolved. Germany is, in effect, a one-party state

1934
June: In the "Night of the Long Knives," Hitler destroys the storm trooper leadership and eliminates opponents
August: After Hindenburg's death, Hitler takes over all his powers. He becomes commander-in-chief of the German armed forces

GLOSSARY

anti-Semitism Religious and racial prejudice against Jews.

Center Party A moderate conservative party, closely linked to the Catholic Church.

chancellor The leading minister under the Weimar Constitution, chosen by the president.

coalition government A government made up of an alliance between political parties.

Communism A political movement advocating the equal division of resources.

Depression, the The worldwide economic collapse between 1929 and 1932, which hit Germany especially hard.

dictatorship A state under the domination of a single leader.

Enabling Act A law passed by the Reichstag in March 1933 enabling Hitler to rule without the Reichstag or other restraint.

fascism Italian political movement founded by Benito Mussolini in the early 1920s that shared many values with the Nazis, including antidemocratic beliefs.

führer Leader.

Gestapo A Nazi police force established by Göring.

inflation A general increase in prices and fall in the purchasing value of money.

proportional representation An election system in which seats are allocated to parties in proportion to the number of votes they gain.

Reichstag German parliament.

Social Democratic Party Non-communist left-wing party.

SS (*Schutzstaffel*) Founded as Hitler's bodyguards, they later became a major instrument of repression and terror.

storm troopers Uniformed Nazi party members used to keep order and intimidate opponents. Also known as the SA from their German name *Sturmabteilung*.

Third Reich The name given to Hitler's state to link it to two earlier German "Reichs" or states: those of Charlemagne, the first Holy Roman Emperor, and Bismarck, the creator of the unified German state (1871).

Weimar Constitution The German system of democratic government from 1919–1933.

FURTHER INFORMATION

Books:

Altman, Linda Jacobs. *Hitler's Rise to Power and the Holocaust*. Berkeley Heights, NJ: Enslow, 2003.

Bartoletti, Susan Campbell. *Hitler Youth*. New York: Scholastic, 2005.

Damon, Duane. *Mein Kampf: Hitler's Blueprint for Aryan Supremacy*. San Diego: Lucent, 2003.

Web Sites:

Germany: Establishment of the Nazi Dictatorship (www.ushmm.org/wlc/en article.php?ModuleId=10005204)

Holocaust Timeline: The Rise of the Nazi Party (fcit.usf.eduHOLOCAUSTTIMELINE/ nazirise.HTM)

Nazi Germany (www.historylearningsite.co.uk/ Nazi%20Germany.htm)

The Rise of Adolf Hitler (www.historyplace. com/worldwar2/riseofhitler)

INDEX

Numbers in **bold** refer to pictures